"I have always admired those who can write short poems, well, and Beth Gulley does not disappoint in her book, *Dragon Eggs*, Spartan Press, 2021. Beth's poems exemplify the skill it takes to write a short poem that perfectly encapsulates image, narrative, flow, and perspective. For example, "The Shooter," captures so much about childhood in its crisp description of a child's marble. Gulley intersperses very tiny poems, with short poems and prose poems shaped in squares. For all of the littleness of the poems, they cover large territories from international atrocities to love of family, childhood, and maturation, as well as delightfully concrete spiritual moments. Her longer poems at the end of the book, "I Am From" and "The New Mythology," are like a genealogy, providing the reader with the collection's roots."

- Phyllis Becker

"Whether in memory-swept narrative poems, or haiku that pack body blows inside of just a few syllables, *Dragon Eggs* delivers masterful verse and sage insight. Beth Gulley finds and elevates the smallest grains of human experience. From classrooms to art museums, from burning prairies to garages turned deathbeds, she carves wisdom from life's best attempts at itself and turns them into verse we can all connect to. Afterall, as the poet points out, "Things like this make great poems, don't they?"

-Timothy Tarkelly, EIC of Stubborn Mule Press

"Beth Gulley's new poetry collection, Dragon Eggs, gives us snapshots of the life of someone who has traveled widely and remained open to experiences in strange places such as El Salvador, Nepal, and Kansas. The title appears in a phrase in the poem "Simplicity," in which the author's sons pick up quartz rocks on a beach and pretend they are dragons' eggs and are "soooo happy." Those who read these mostly brief, accessible, understated, deceptively simple poems will be rewarded by finding many gems throughout and will also find delight. The range of experience presented is impressive as are the writer's fresh observations. In the final poem, "The New Mythology," she writes about her grandfather's sorrow over the loss of a child and of his happiness at her (the author's) birth. The first grandchild, she is "the jewel in the new mythology." Throughout the book many gems in the experiences that make up her developing mythology glimmer."

-Patricia Lawson

"In *Dragon Eggs*, Beth Gulley faithfully follows William Zinsser's advice for writing memoir: "Memoir isn't the summary of a life; it's a window into a life." In this straightforward collection, Gulley recounts memories from childhood in war-torn El Salvador, the joys and frustrations of motherhood, and with a reporter's eye, the unfolding of events that's she's observed. Sometimes her voice is philosophical; sometimes it campaigns for social justice; sometimes her voice is delightfully sassy and self-deprecating."

-Rikki Santer, *Stopover* (Luchador Press, 2021)

Dragon Eggs

Poems by Beth Gulley

Spartan Press
Kanasas City, Missouri
spartanpress.com

Copyright © Beth Gulley, 2021
First Edition: 1 3 5 7 9 10 8 6 4 2
ISBN: 978-1-952411-71-7
LCCN: 2021944937

Cover image: Alex Whitney
Author photo: Jeremy Gulley
All rights reserved. No part of this publication may be reproduced or transmitted in any form or by any means, electronic or mechanical, including photocopying, recording or by info retrieval system, without prior written permission from the author.

Acknowledgmments:

"Open Happiness" appeared for the first time in the 2015 issue of *The Same*.

A version of "Company" was previously published in *The Flint Hills Review* in 2013.

"Company," "My Eighth Grade English Teacher," "Hydroelectric," and "Handwashing Part One: A Childhood Memory" were published in *$!*#hole Countries: A Find and Replace Meditation* in 2018.

"Roadkill" first appeared in *365 Days: A Poetry Anthology* in 2016.

"It Was Supposed to Be an Academic Discussion about Homelessness," "FERPA Violation," and "Newsflash: Johnny's Teacher Can't Play Nice" first appeared in the 2015 edition of *Kansas English*.

Also, special thanks to the Collaborators, the 365 Poetry Facebook group, the Riverfront Reading Group, the Writers Place, and the Kansas Authors Club. As always, I am thankful for my family who read all my early drafts and who always support and inspire me. And special thanks to Alex for the beautiful cover art.

Table of Contents:

Company / 1

Coca-Cola / 2

My Eighth Grade English Teacher / 3

Hydroelectric / 4

Hand Washing Part One: A childhood memory / 5

Hand Washing Part Two: Employees
   Must Wash Hands before Returning to Work / 6

Hand Washing Part Three: Audacity / 7

Police Lights at a Small Town Intersection / 8

Easter Sunday / 9

I Don't Eat Last / 10

Simplicity / 11

Boys Fish / 12

Two Dimes / 13

It Was Supposed to Be an Academic
   Discussion about Homelessness / 14

FERPA Violation / 15

Newsflash: Johnny's Teacher Can't Play Nice / 16

Poem of Conversation Regarding a
   Plane Ticket Found in a Book / 17

13901 W. 56th Terrace / 18

For Josh—(Because He Sees) / 19

On His First Day as a Tour Guide
   at the Thomas Hart Benton House / 20

To the Woman in Texas Who Ran over
   a Homeless Man, Took Him Home, and
   Let Him Die in Her Garage / 21

When the War and the Earthquake Don't Take You / 22

Her Presence / 23

Please Step Away from the Painting / 24

Bowling / 25

Night Lights / 26

Agra Tourism / 27

The Shooter / 28

Communitarianism—the Downside / 29

Apostate / 30

First World Confidence / 31

Faker / 33

Did You Know the Sun Is Shining? / 34

Tomato Plant / 35

Rejection Letter / 36

On the Lawn of the Nelson Atkins
   Museum of Art / 37

September 11, 1973 / 38

Wonder: A Memory / 39

After 5 Months—Missing My Son / 40

Feedback / 41

Fiction Forsaken / 42

YIKES! / 43

Open Happiness / 44

Autocorrect / 44

Do You Have a Line for Me? / 45

They Are Wearing Plastic Pants / 46

Evil—She's so Sexy / 47

Don't Waste Words / 48

Thin Place / 49

Conversion Chart / 50

Public Service Announcement / 51

My Legs / 52

Breathe / 53

What Is the Next Song? / 54

The Only One Knowing It / 55

This Time It's Personal / 56

Curb / 57

Finally / 58

Great Weekend . . . / 59

Self-Purification (You Went All Dr. King on Me) / 60

The Only Person to Have Seen This Monster
   Is a Person Named Asher Gulley / 61

Can You Give Me a Minute? / 62

Austin Rivers Is on Fire! / 63

Jeans / 64

Free Entry / 65

Cars without Race Stickers / 66

Adam Named the World / 67

Nepal / 68

So…I have so many things I don't want to grade… / 69

I Dreamt / 70

At the Kansas Prairie Grass Burn / 71

Road Kill / 72

I Am From / 73

The New Mythology / 74

*Some old-fashioned things like fresh air
and sunshine are hard to beat.*

- Laura Ingalls Wilder

for Jeremy, Israel, and Asher
And for my mom who can do anything
and who holds all things together.

Company

It's drizzling out,
and the TV news is supposed to keep me company,
but like always
it just holds up a mirror
 to a little girl I have tried to patch up
into an adult.

Military helicopters evacuate U.S. citizens from Albania
--mostly children—
and seven school girls were gunned down in Israel today
while on a class trip.

Flashback—
I'm eleven.
It's three in the morning in San Salvador,
And helicopters are flying low over the maid's quarters
   where we sleep.
I hear bombs explode in the city,
but Kelly says,
"Go back to sleep. It's just the war."

Coca-Cola

"I still remember the airline stewardess' response to my parents when they found out they were taking three little children to El Salvador in August of 1984," my sister wrote in her diversity statement on her application to Georgetown school of International Law. The memory of our trip struck me as I was proofreading for her. This was the moment we realized our trip was not mundane. That flight let us out in Miami airport where we wandered over to TACA to board our first international flight. The average passenger's height dropped a foot, and the boom box won "the most popular piece of carry-on luggage" contest. The squall of Spanish pushed us on the TACA tube at one end, and slowly squeezed us like toothpaste into an alternative reality. At the San Salvador airport, the customs officials opened all our suitcases and rifled all our stuff. They laughed at my little brother's stuffed buffalo and let us through without a bribe. As the sliding doors opened, dirty little children sang us *da me cinco,* and we were hustled into a white van. The sun was setting over banana plants and tin roofs. When we turned a corner, we saw a giant Coca-Cola billboard. I began to relax my grip on my teddy bear, and I thought, maybe this would be ok.

My Eighth Grade English Teacher

My eighth grade English teacher,
Chris Babcock,
got blown up by a Molotov cocktail.
(Word came in a letter.)

He didn't listen.
The Embassy said
everyone should stay put,
but Chris elected
to drive home
where he arrived
at the same time
 some Salvadoran crazies
threw
a bomb
in his garage
in protest of
 the newly installed government.

Hydroelectric

On our field trip to the hydroelectric plant,
I remember squishing in next to Kelly
on the dirty black floor of the white Toyota hi-ace van.

I remember the acrid chili pepper smell
of fresh coffee beans drying on
the straight reflective lines on the road.

I remember getting peanut butter stuck
to the roof of my mouth
and washing it down with
fizzy stingy coca cola before
running to play hide and seek on
the rough ancient unprotected Maya ruin,
the slap of my sandals against the stone.

I do not remember the hydroelectric plant.

Hand Washing Part One: A childhood memory

After three days of water rationing,
no one remembered
who twisted the faucet on,
found no water,
and failed to twist it off.

So there was no one to blame
when at four a.m.
the water came back on,
and by five a.m.
a two inch pool formed
from the kitchen to the bedrooms.

For the first time
we were grateful
for the cold tile floors
and push mops.

Hand Washing Part Two:
Employees Must Wash Hands Before
Returning to Work

Every time I wash my hands
in a public restroom
I think of Jimmy Wang
who, in 5th grade, got
Hepatitis A
and peed in the soap dispenser.

Hand Washing Part Three: Audacity

The day care teacher
squirts soft soap
into ten tiny palms,
not realizing
she has tipped her hand
revealing herself
as someone who has never
turned the faucet
and found it wanting.

Unfortunately,
today is her "lucky" day,
and now she has to regroup
as ten toddlers touch
each other
with soapy hands.

Frantically she attempts
to find an alternative method
for soap removal
while keeping her charges in line
 in a public park.

Police Lights at a Small Town Intersection

"Are they blocking traffic
for a flat tire?"

"Oh, GOD, it's a bicycle!"
Lodged like a jack
beneath
the driver's side back tire.

We saw no child
we saw no ambulance

 but a new sense of gratitude
lodged in my chest
as my own son,
a block later,
stepped safely to the curb
and entered the school.

Easter Sunday

Behind me
a man audibly harasses his ex-wife
while their 5 and 3 year old
sit between them.

On the stage
a woman performs a monologue
of Mary Magdalene
at the tomb.

And I am caught
between "the restraining order says. . ."
and
"Let he who is without sin cast the first stone."

I Don't Eat Last

I don't eat last.
It sets me apart
from those "nice" ladies who serve
everyone else first and just take
what is left while the three-
year-old across the table eats
four bites of the steak/roll/pie
they really want and then feeds
the rest to the garbage disposal.

No. I don't eat last.
I take what I really want.
And if what I really want is gone,
I go to the store and buy some more.
How silly to sulk about not getting any ice cream
when you are 36, have a car,
a driver's license, and five dollars in cash.
I don't eat last.
I go after what I really want.

Simplicity

The beach house
resembles Laura's house
outside Independence, Kansas
where Mr. Edwards
 brought
Laura and Mary
a penny each
 and a stick of candy
for Christmas,
and they were soooo happy.

We bundle up
And pick up shells
And quartz rocks on the beach.
(The air is too cold to touch,
so swimming is out of the question.)
My boys pretend
the rocks are dragons' eggs,
And they are soooo happy.

Boys Fish

Boys fish
from the rocks
with poles and lures,
but catch only
sweat beads
and itchy legs.

Two Dimes

"When I came back in from recess, I found two dimes on my desk," Israel said as he got in the car. "I turned them in to my teacher, but she tried to give them back to me at the end of the day." "So you have two dimes?" I tried to fill in the blank. "No. Just because we don't know who those dimes belong to doesn't mean they belong to me," Israel responded. "Grandma (the school secretary) said she would keep them in her desk until the end of the year to see if anyone comes back for them." All my life I thought I was a moral person, until now. My five year old son's clarity about what did and did not belong to him, and what was and was not significant, cut me to the quick. I would have taken those two dimes, and I would have spent them on a vending machine snack. Seven years later, when Grandma retired from the school district, the two dimes were still in her desk. And my son still refused to take something that didn't belong to him. And I am still awed that he cares that much about doing right, even when the adults around him try to talk him out of listening to his conscience.

It was supposed to be an academic discussion about homelessness.

It was supposed to be an academic discussion
    about homelessness.

A gray haired presenter stood—coffee in hand—
    at the front table,
fielding questions about the shelter he directs.

But the "preambles" to students' questions grew longer and
    longer
(when I was an addict and my mom kicked me out…).

Until Karen's "question" wobbled out of her mouth,
—Do you help people with their utilities?—
and her tear stream indicated she meant
--Can you help ME with My utilities?—

Then from across the room
Three other girls quietly snaked a box of tissues to Karen
--as if to say—
You are not invisible to us.

FERPA Violation

As she reads from a statement
she confesses later that her mother wrote
(even though it is written in the first person)
it is painfully clear
that this young lady
is not on her way to Freshman Comp, Spanish II, or
    Microbiology.
(or even a career as an administrative assistant)

Her helper touches her arm
on the elbow and repeats
any question we ask her.

Her answers seem rehearsed
especially when she is asked
"Why are you in college?"
and she says
"I'm going to work very hard."

Newsflash: Johnny's Teacher Can't Play Nice

Students shook my hand
two days in a row for kind
acts they should expect.

Poem of conversation regarding a plane ticket found in a book

You should write a poem about this

No – You should

It's your ticket

It was in your book – I never read that book

It was just a – what do you call those things – a bookmark – I had to use something

Hey, it's from our trip to Chicago

I remember that

When you almost got thrown off the plane – what was it 2002? – for making remarks about the explosives in your shoes

Yeah, remember, we rode the train and saw an old man actually reading music?

And accidentally saw Studs Terkell open for Grace Paley

Things like this make great poems, don't they?

Yeah, you should write a poem about this.

13901 W. 56th Terrace

Goodbye little house—
monument to resisting change.
You were the original house
in a neighborhood where 1950s ranch styles
grew up around you like dandelions
infiltrate a patch of violets.
My toddler found your well--
hastily filled in after running water
came from the city.
Even though some crazy boys once
drove their motorcycles inside of you,
your solid oak beams and brick/stone structure
were not shaken.
We don't want change.
But now our two boys
are too big for one room.
They are young—they need change.
Even though we tried to sabotage
our pre-approved mortgage,
the faxes come in,
our mortgage still stands,
our offer is accepted.
We must change.
Our young boys lead us out
while our feet are still dragging,
and we leave you
a monument—but someone else's scenery.

For Josh—
(because he sees)

*This poem is in regards to the Occupy Cal Protest on November 9, 2011 at U.C. Berkley during which many students and professors were beaten by police.

Ten years ago
Josh Anderson bore witness
to my deepest shame
when he called out to me
while I was quickly pushing my baby stroller
 away from the homeless.
So intent on pretending not to see
that I didn't see him just sitting there
among the rejected.

Ten days ago
Josh Anderson bore witness
to our nation's deepest shame
when as a graduate student
at U.C. Berkley, he called out
to the Board of Regents
and the Riot Police could only see
a mob, and they beat him until
he could not get up,
for peacefully protesting an 81% tuition increase.

On His First Day as a Tour Guide at the Thomas Hart Benton House

On his first day as a tour guide
his mom arrived at the gate
as arranged, along with four unexpected guests.
(Where did they come from?
Four people on a rainy Monday?)

He felt good about not stuttering
even though he forgot a few important details
about the historic house.
And he repeated the bit about
the famous painter dying
eleven weeks before his stubborn, savvy wife
once in the garden and twice in the studio.

But the tourists all said "thank you"
even though they didn't exactly look
like they were listening.
At least they didn't ask any questions.

To the Woman in Texas Who Ran Over a Homeless Man, Took Him Home, and Let Him Die in Her Garage:

I was hungry,
and you drove over me.

I was homeless,
and you drove me home
stuck in your windshield.

I was thirsty,
and you drowned me
with empty apologies.

I was bleeding,
and you left me in your car
for three days.

I was alone,
and your actions
joined our names in the headlines.

I could have been the Christ,
yet you lacked the humanity
to remain at the scene of the accident.

Her Presence

Her presence practically
rends the universe,
but she leaves an empty
tear when she's gone.

Please Step Away from the Painting

From someone whose hair
crudely brushed a Van Gough (oops)
--docents are useful.

Bowling

I'm the kind of girl
bigoted bowling pins hate.
They split to mock me.

Night Lights

Pictures of faraway nebula
lose out over fireworks
100 feet away.

Agra Tourism

If you put a fan on
your wind chimes,
are you cheating?

The Shooter

Cloudy
sparkly
ocean blue sphere
metallic
click plop
in the jar
slick and salty
with the sweaty
little boy's
fingers
the smell of purple gum
and luck.

Communitarianism—the Downside

But hey. Yanking my boy around on a monkey leash at the zoo was supposed to work out for me. That way I wouldn't have to reinjure my back leaning over his stroller the whole time, and he could run up close and look at the animals. But he kept running away from me. So I would yank hard on the leash, and then that little brat would fall down. I got so mad; I just screamed at him to get up. People around me started to whisper. I knew they were talking about me. Then one of those busy body ladies, who thinks her way of parenting is the only way of parenting, clicked over in her two inch heels (at the zoo now mind you) to the security guard, and almost spilled her latte on him she was so intent on squealing to him that I was abusing my child. Now I am stuck in this hot office answering annoying questions.

Apostate

I am a non-believer
in a room filled with
sanctified holy fitness gurus
who plan to evangelize the world
with the message of
Cycle Reebok
through the gospel
of Walk-Talk-and-Tone.
My cynicism brings anger
to their cholesterol free hearts.
How could any red blooded American
not worship at the shrine
of her own body?

First World Confidence

Kinsey thought she knew everything,
but she never saw the beautiful almond eyed baby
with welts on her head, and welts on her back,
playing in the stick hut in a coastal town
even Coca Cola couldn't find.
Or she would have realized
some things are unfathomable.

Faker

So much for all of my self-righteous talk.
It was all big words trying to conceal a dirty heart.

I've played that game well.
I'm smart enough
to know what you get
when you fall down.
You get kicked in the teeth.

But isn't it worse.
I've talked about other people selling out
in that arrogant voice.
Now me wearing the name Faker
across my heart.

Like one of those big
cheezer convention stickers
"Hello, My Name is Faker."

"Is that an Arab name?" they might ask.
Oh no, it's just that my soul was dirty
And I didn't have time to wash it,
So I just covered it up with make-up
And doused the perfume.

It's just my luck.
I fell of the boat,
And everything washed off.
Someone on board was yelling
"Hey, Jonah!"

Did you know the sun is shining?

Did you know the sun is shining?
Drinking deeply at the pool of reflection
we inhale ourselves
over and over
around and around.
This nectar inside our stomachs
causes us
to embrace ourselves as the fittest
then to beat ourselves with hooked lashes.
We are never really satisfied
until we stop drinking
and look up at the sun.

Tomato plant

I bought the mostly
wilted ten inch leafy plant
from Wal-Mart for 10 cents
and thought it would probably die
but was worth a try.

I dug a hole
in the dark, rocky, grassy ground
by the hot silver colored fence,
to the smell of musty wet upturned earth.

Oh, the cold, sweet, juicy taste of ripe tomatoes.

Rejection Letter

"You got a rejection letter," he said,
waving a plain white envelope with no return address.

I slice it open to find a news clipping and a sticky note
--an ad from someone who signed only "J."

So yes, I got a letter to reject.
The more common, less painful kind of rejection.

On the Lawn of the Nelson Atkins Museum of Art

She turns from
the headless statues
like she turns from
the toothless man
in front of McDonald's.
Like she turns off
the documentary on
sex slavery in Thailand.

Like she turned from
the blind woman who had
burn scars in her hair.

As if by turning her head
she could turn the world.

September 11, 1973

On September 11, 1973
over 3,000 people disappeared
in Santiago de Chile.
People—like little leaves
shaken from trees,
scraped together,
then dumped--
Their distorted bodies
floating down river.
Another Historical Moment
sponsored by
The Strength of a Few
to remind the many
We Are Not Safe.

Wonder: A memory

Me, in a size small white sweater,
skipping from the classroom
across the quad to the office
on an errand for my first grade teacher
while pink sunrays scatter.

After 5 Months—Missing My Son

Running
too quick
for heart
sick.
Mud
trips
me
up
long
enough
for heart ache
to catch up.

Feedback

Mrs. Weatherbie,
my son wrote in his journal
that he was sitting next to his Papa
when his Papa died.
My son told you
this was very hard for him.
You responded simply
by writing −10 at the top.

What part of watching
someone you love die merits a −10?
Or did you mean on a scale of 1-10,
1 being the most painful,
my son must have endured
pain beyond the scale?

We can't tell.
All you wrote was −10.

Fiction Forsaken

Book stacks by the bed
accuse.
Ideas abandoned
too early. . .
shame me.

YIKES!

Yoga breathing
only gets
you half way
there.

Sometimes
mind control
only works
on others.

Open Happiness

In a place where
I can't read or speak
and even the toilets
don't make sense,
Coca-Cola still
tastes like home.

Autocorrect

Autocorrect
moves beyond
the realm of spelling
to tackle
immoral behavior.

Try it today.
Watch Tax Evasion
become
Flax Invasion
before your very eyes.

Do you have a line for me?

Do you have a line for me?
I want to fish in the neighbor's
pond for stocked bass
and make stew out of the poor turtle
that gets caught on the hook.
Share a line.
Let me stand
beside you
in the sun.

They Are Wearing Plastic Pants

Let's table
the plastic pants
discussion
for now.
We have
a more pressing
problem
with middle aged
women
wearing
Capri tights
to Walmart.

Evil—She's So Sexy

Ending with Nazi propaganda
is always the way to go
when you want to drive home
that evil dresses like a beautiful woman.

Don't Waste Words

It is important
to have the right person
in front of you,
or all of those silvery words
will wind back on you
and choke you.

Thin Place

--For Peter Gomes

Thin places
between heaven
and earth
sometimes
wear open
if we tread
them often

Conversion Chart

My notebook has a conversion chart
for feet to meters, Fahrenheit to Celsius,
and pounds to kilograms,
but there is no chart to convert
my love for you into anything else.
You are going to have to take it for what it is.

Public Service Announcement

If any strange person
asks you to hold
their emotional baggage,
immediately report it
to the highest authorities.

This may be done
by prostrating yourself,
crossing yourself, or chanting,
but a simple "God help me"
will do.

My Legs

My legs
still work
even though
they carry
scars--
many more
than when
I was 12.

But to fixate
on the flaws
is to miss
the point.
My legs
work
really well.

Breathe

Blanket to chin with
knees tucked in. Nothing to do
till Monday but breathe.

What Is the Next Song?

How bout you play
the one about
you and me
selling all our stuff,
running off, and living
like educated gypsies.
The one where we
love each other forever
in a tiny world
we created ourselves...
That one.

The Only One Knowing It

Something's killing Keaty.
She won't even name it.
But she came to class
to tell us
cause she didn't want to be
the only one knowing it.

This Time It's Personal

Are you really going to root
against James Hardin?
After you dropped the Thunder
when they cut him loose?
The man with the beard
stands out
because he cares...
and eventually you will too.

Curb

Ever since my dog
walked my foot
into a curb,
the scrape and
the bruise
cleared my mind
of other worries.

Finally

I'm obsessed with how
you will react when I die--
take it extra hard!

Great Weekend...

My car looks like
I mistook it
for a birthday cake
and coated it
thick with chocolate frosting.

Self Purification (You went all Dr King on me!)

Did you get your question answered?
Are you prepared for the answer to be no?
Are you able to accept blow without retaliation?
Are you prepared to be shamed? To be killed?
Self purification--an important part of daily preparation.

"The only person to have seen this monster is a person named Asher Gulley"

Since his feet
don't touch the floor,
he can swing
side to side
in my office chair
while drawing
a monster
with red and blue
markers
and acting out
the scene
on giant paper.
I brought my son
to my office,
but he was
too compelled
by his inner world
to notice.

Can You Give Me A Minute?

Can you give me a minute?
Maybe listen with your mouth closed?
In the known-new contract
the new information comes at the end.

Austin Rivers Is on Fire!

Chris Paul
assists his coach
by giving him
permission
to be proud
of his son.

Jeans

This morning I found a book
on the floor and I flipped
it open to a poem about jeans
that was not about jeans, but loss.
I thought, what luck to stumble
on insight so early in the day.

Free Entry

An estate sale
in the rich neighborhood.
Nice! Free entry
into a fancy house.
Tiny on the inside
it turns out
and the flooring
all ripped out.
Funny the feeling
of gratitude for my
old two story
on a corner lot.

Cars without Race Stickers

Cars without
race stickers
line up
like sixlets.
Runners
In race shirts
find their
wave starts.
At the Corporate
Five K
I cross
alone.

Adam Named the World

Adam named the world,
and Eve came along
and suggested
he would like it better
if he used her words instead.

Nepal

The Swiss earthquake team
always arrives first
because the world
cares enough
to send the very best.

So…I have so many things I don't want to grade…

Feedback
Frozen
Papers
Packed
Still
Unread
Pain
Self
Inflicted
Resolution
Simple
Simply
Stalled.

I Dreamt

I dreamt
they wouldn't
serve me
any coffee.
I woke
in terror!

At the Kansas Institute Prairie Grass Burn

When I lit the prairie grass
with a match and watched tufts
of it spark and char,
I wanted to time travel
and tell 8 year old me
that a day would come
when I could play with matches
at work on someone's sculpture,
and a reporter from the Star
would take my picture,
and the artist would shake my hand.

Road Kill

Just because
I can't see
the corpse
of the dog
I hit this morning
doesn't mean
the accident
was a dream.
But I can
pretend.

I Am From

I am from David and Beverly,
 Charles and Allie, Everett and Doris
From wheat fields at sunset
And hibiscus at sunrise
I am from French fries and ice cream
From punk rock and poetry
From the tiny Christian Church
With real live Indians smoking out front.
I am from "God will take care of you"
And "Victory in Jesus."
From the missionaries who gave up
The house they built
With their inheritance money
In order to make peace.
I am from the red dirt of Paraguay
And the earthquake cracked buildings of San Salvador.
I am from choir trips to the beach,
From Coca-Cola and hermit crabs.
From the Delta airlines flight
That made sure my father's coffin
Arrived safely in Arkansas.
From the scientific diligence in my grandmother's notebooks
And the spiritual surrender in my grandfather's poems.
And I can see that I was always loved.

The New Mythology

Out the window red dots flashed straight up into the night sky between Heston and Newton in Central Kansas. I leaned my head against the window. My little brother already fell asleep, and my dad grew tired of talking so instead of telling me a story he popped in a cassette tape of my Grandpa Gruver telling his life story.

The tape started at the part about the little family he stayed with in China sometime after language school but sometime before he converted the bandits up near Mongolia. "They didn't have much furniture," he reported, "just the word Jesus written in chalk on the wall. They had a little child. A sweet little child. But when I visited again later the child had died."

As a child myself, I did not have a frame of reference to pin my grandfather's experience to. He seemed so sad on this part of the tape. He paused, and then he moved on to a happier time. Losing this child seemed to have been hard for him. Maybe unexplainable.

As we passed the last wheat field and pulled into town, I pretended to be asleep so my dad would carry me into the house. My grandfather's voice sank into my psyche and his stories began to form a mythology in my head. And his friends had lost a precious child, but when he was 80 I was born . . . a precious child . . . the first grandchild . . . the jewel in the new mythology.

Beth Gulley lives in Spring Hill, Kansas and teaches writing at Johnson County Community College. She has an MA from UMKC and a PhD from the University of Kansas. When not writing about teaching, Beth primarily writes poetry.She in 2018 published a chapbook, *$!*# Hole Countries: A Find and Replace Meditation.* Her work also appears in the *Bards Against Hunger Anthology, From Everywhere a Little: A Migration Anthology,* the *Thorny Locust,* and *The Gasconade Review Presents: Storm A'Comin', Kansas Letters to a Young Poet,* and the *105 Meadowlark Reader.* She has been a proud member of the Facebook group 365 Poems in 365 Days since 2015, and her poems appear in all three of the 365 Poems in 365 Days anthologies. Beth serves on the Riverfront Reading Committee and is a Writer's Place board member. She loves thrift store shopping, traveling, and drinking coffee.

www.ingramcontent.com/pod-product-compliance
Lightning Source LLC
Chambersburg PA
CBHW030345100526
44592CB00010B/834